*L*oving *Your* Long-Distance Relationship

Stephen Blake

D1115169

Anton
Anton Publishing * Canada

Published by
Anton Publishing
305 Madison Ave.
Suite 1166
New York, New York 10165

Cover art by: Those wacky Rickner Brothers (Adam &
Sean). You can reach them at www.escape.ca/~srickner

Printed in Canada.

ISBN 0-9680971-0-3

To the Sherbrooks,

For their undying challenge, inspiration, guidance, support, and love.

I dedicate this book to you.

Contents

Introduction

I start crying as the airplane moves away from the terminal. Wiping a tear, I recall what a wonderful time that I have just spent with my girlfriend. The picture is so vivid that I can feel her in my arms, hear her whisper in my ear, and taste her lips tenderly pressed against mine. My heart fills with the emotions that we share when we are together . . . laughing, talking, making love.

Suddenly the roar of an airplane distracts me. Realizing that my feelings are nothing more than a daydream, and that my girlfriend is on a flight travelling thousands of miles away from me, I start crying again. As her plane ascends, I am reminded that I will not see her for several weeks or even months, and that when we do meet again, it may be only for a few days. Now I feel angry, wondering why she cannot be beside me all the time. Why must I endure an emotional roller coaster every time I step into an airport? I start blaming myself for ever being in such a relationship. Then, as I watch her plane being consumed by an afternoon sunset, the vision returns of the wonderful time we have just spent together and how much we love each other. At once, everything seems worthwhile and the only thing that matters is rushing home to wait by the phone for her call. Turning to leave the terminal, I try to conceal my tears from curious strangers. I know that they do not know me but in some odd way, they understand.

Does this sound familiar? If not, substitute the word "boyfriend," "wife," or "husband" for "girlfriend." If this still doesn't sound familiar, replace the word "train" for "airplane." How's that? More familiar? If so, you are probably in a long-distance relationship. You deeply love someone, but for some reason you must be apart from them for an extended period. Maybe you chose to attend university in a different country than your partner. Perhaps they accepted a job in another city because the same opportunity did not exist in the city in which you live. What if you just want to live in another country for a year or two to expand your horizons?

You know that you love your partner and that both of you will grow more by being apart temporarily. Yet your heart feels like it is breaking and you wonder how you are ever going to survive being alone without losing your mind. I know the feeling. As I write this book, I face two more years of separation from my girlfriend, Amanda. We both love each other deeply, but because she could not find a local university that offered a graduate degree in her field of interest, we both agreed that she should study in another city--1500 miles away. This was the right choice, because I know her education will make her feel more secure and fulfilled. At the same time, I also realize that I am going to miss her terribly.

This is my third serious long-distance relationship so I know what to expect. Despite how much I love Amanda, I can expect to feel lonely. I can expect the only real contact I will have with her will be a daily ten or twenty minute conversation on the phone. I also can expect that when I am down, certain people or even my own imagination will try to sabotage my faith in my relationship.

Realizing that I must be apart from Amanda and knowing what to expect in her absence, I can spend my time in two ways. I can wallow in self-pity and let every challenge that arises while she is gone get me down. Or I can focus on how happy I am that she is enriching herself, trying my best to anticipate and overcome the challenges that distance will create in our relationship.

As you might have guessed, I chose the latter. Unlike my past two long-distance relationships, I am committed to being happy while we are apart. However, I realize that commitment is only the start. If I want to be truly happy, I must anticipate the challenges in my relationship, and decide how to meet them with a positive emotional and mental spirit.

In the following pages you will find some stories that illustrate the obstacles that I faced being apart from a loved one. You will also find several insights describing some simple things that I did to overcome those difficulties. Please know that they are not cure-alls for the problems in every relationship, close or long-distance. They are simply what helps me from going completely insane from missing Amanda. I know you don't know me personally, but please trust that I am trying to do all that I can to be happier while being apart from her. After all, you can try a lot of things in two years if you put your mind to it.

As you read this book, I hope that you will feel

like you are having a conversation with a friend. A friend who is in a long-distance relationship and wants to share his feelings on how he did his best to be happy for twenty-four months while being apart from the woman he loves. I also hope that this book comforts you. I hope it reassures you that you aren't alone, and that people everywhere are experiencing the same emotions you are. Long-distance isn't the end of the world, and if you have the desire, you can be just as happy apart from your loved one as when you are together. If your loved one is like my girlfriend, I know that they would feel better knowing that you are happy while they're away. Even if you aren't in a long-distance relationship, chances are that you know someone who is, and may be looking for some support. Whatever your reason for reading this book, I offer you some stories and insights that if only to dry your eyes for an hour or two, were worth sharing.

Coping With Having to Say Goodbye Again and Again

It never fails. A week or two before Amanda goes back to university, a mysterious anxiety seems to surround our every move. We both know our time together was beautiful. We took long walks together, visited each other's family, and talked about how wonderful it will be when we are finally together--permanently. Nevertheless, two weeks before she plans to leave, we feel tense. Unlike the beginning of her stay, we feel an invisible wall coming between us. The smallest things, like what courses she will be taking, turn into disagreements. Although we cannot control our emotions, we realize that we are wasting the precious little time that we have left together.

If you are in, or have been in a long-distance relationship, you probably know exactly what I am talking about. If you have endured countless goodbyes, you probably realize that the feelings you experience before your loved one leaves, arise from you anticipating how much it will hurt once they go. Whether I like it or not, about two weeks before Amanda departs, I cannot help thinking about how sad I am going to feel in the airport kissing her for the last time. Or how lonely I am going to feel on the weekend when I realize that our only time together will be a short phone conversation. Or how her leaving this time may mean the end of our relationship.

I don't even want to think of the time I have wasted in the past, feeling upset about a girlfriend leaving town. No matter how much I prepared for those troubling thoughts and feelings, I knew they would come. I would let my emotions consume me and spoil the time we had left. Looking back, I think I enjoyed feeling upset . . . in a warped sort of way. I felt entitled to feel bad, and would deliberately upset my girlfriend as a reward to myself for what I would have to endure in a few weeks. It's crazy what the mind and heart will do if you let them!

About a month ago, before Amanda left town we committed to make her last two weeks just as special as her first two (though we are true believers in letting emotions take their course). I am proud to say the experiment worked! For the first time in my life, I experienced very little anxiety in the time before her departure. I didn't even feel crushed at the airport. We both felt calm and secure in her leaving, and we avoided putting any emotional walls between us to insulate ourselves from being hurt. Sound interesting? Here's how we did it.

We found a good way to feel more secure was to make some long-term plans. We didn't sit and plan in detail what we were going to do with the rest of our lives. I think that's unrealistic and would be a waste of time in our last two weeks together. What we did do, was talk about when we would be together next, how long her stay would be at her university, and what we planned to do when she returned.

We, of course, knew all of this before she left. The goal in talking about our future, however, wasn't to make new plans, but to give each other the feeling that despite the time we had to be apart, we would eventually be together. After talking about how wonderful our future was going to be, a short term absence from each other seemed insignificant by comparison. All that mattered was being together again as soon as possible. How or when we would be together was not an issue. We both knew we had to make it, or the hope of being together permanently would be lost.

No matter how strong our relationship is, I eventually hear about another long-distance relationship that has failed and I wonder if we will suffer the same fate. The last time I heard one of these stories was from Amanda a few weeks before she left town. At a dinner one night, she described how a guy she knew had a girlfriend who went to Russia on an exchange program. They had gone out for several years and were planning to be married. Yet only weeks before she was to return home, she called her boyfriend and informed him that she had met someone else, she was staying away longer than anticipated, and that her plans for marrying him were over. Right out of the blue. Wham! Just when he was looking forward to picking her up from the airport in a few weeks.

Anyway, given that Amanda was leaving shortly, she and I could have used this story as a perfect opportunity to start doubting our own relationship by asking those dreaded "yes, but what if . . . " questions. Instead, we used the story as an opportunity to reassure each other of what wouldn't happen in our relationship and how much we loved each other. We used the story as an example of what not to do, pledging never to let the same thing happen to us. We both came to the conclusion that this couple shared problems that had nothing to do with long-distance. They had problems such as a lack of commitment and trust that we didn't have, and would never contemplate having. After our conversation ended, we both felt stronger and reassured, knowing that we loved each other and were committed to our relationship . . . no matter what. This was a tremendous feeling of love and security to share with each other before she left town.

If I know Amanda is leaving in a couple of weeks I will change my schedule so I can spend more time with her. It's a natural response when you love someone and enjoy being around them as much as possible. Nevertheless, what I have found is that altering my routine significantly triggers something inside me that says Amanda is going and I should feel bad. When I keep different work hours, or see her at different times than I normally would, I start feeling like something is wrong. I feel like it is the beginning of a cycle that will end in hurt and unhappiness. I am not saying that one should not spend more time with their loved one before they leave town, but I have found that it is better not to alter my day drastically before Amanda leaves. The last time she departed, in the preceding weeks I tried to do everything I would do normally as if she wasn't going away. I didn't change my weekly work hours, daily workout routine, etc. I did, however, spend more time with her Friday, Saturday, and Sunday, the days when we would usually spend the most time together during the week if she wasn't leaving.

The result was I did not feel any different in the two weeks before her departure than I did the other four months that we were together. After all, nothing in my daily routine suggested that she was leaving. We both just went about our lives as usual, and as a result we encouraged no feelings of change or impending doom. I would not have believed it myself if someone told me just to act the same as I usually did before Amanda left. I always considered those two or three weeks as a necessary ritual in which I had to change everything and spend as much time with her as possible, trying desperately to absorb as much intimacy and physical contact as I could. I was wrong. What I never realized was that the more my routine changed, the more my feelings did as well. So instead of changing my daily patterns, I will now keep the same routine just before Amanda's departure, along with the same feelings I have for her while we are together the other 99% of the time.

It took me years to learn, but I finally realized it's better not to see a girlfriend just before she leaves town. In other words, I do not say goodbye at the airport anymore. Now before you condemn me for being an unfeeling monster, ask yourself this question: "What happens just before your lover leaves?" From experience, my guess is that you probably feel terrible. No matter what you have tried to do in the weeks leading up to your partner's departure, you just can't help feeling this is the last time you will see your loved one for who knows how long. Consequently, you both cry uncontrollably. You start holding and kissing each other like you will never see each other again. You pledge that you will always love each other, and that you will never forget to call or write. Perhaps you exchange gifts, making the moment even more emotional and intense. You both try to ignore the loud speaker announcing that your lover's plane or train leaves in ten minutes. Finally, you realize that you can be together no longer. Using all of the strength left in your body, you give each other one last kiss, then say goodbye. You both start crying again as your lover walks away. You keep waving, but soon you cannot see each other anymore. You turn and leave the airport crying. You realize that no matter how hard you try, you probably will have a bad day and get nothing done.

One can look at last minute goodbyes from a different perspective. For example, in my first serious long-distance relationship, I believed that if I really loved my girlfriend, I had to endure massive suffering every time she left the city. Not to see her at the last minute of her departure would be like cheating both of us out of the one, final emotional moment that we had left together. If I did not see her off, I risked losing this moment with her forever. Worse, she might not love me any more if I missed her at the airport. I knew I would feel terrible when she left, but compared with the risk and the guilt associated with not seeing her off, the pain of saying goodbye was worth it.

I might have maintained this perspective if farewells only occurred once in awhile, but they didn't. Saying goodbye happened every couple of months, and by the twentieth or so parting, I began to question whether seeing my girlfriend off at the airport was really worth the pain. I started to ask myself what would happen if we didn't see each other for that last hour. Would we love each other any less? Would we feel cheated? Would guilt consume us until we saw each other the next time? As it turns out, none of those things occurred the first time I avoided the airport. In fact, instead of feeling cheated or guilty, we both felt relieved that we could still love each other without having a nervous breakdown every time she left town.

I still avoid the airport in my current

relationship. Instead of crying and clinging to each other while the last few minutes tick away on the terminal's clock, Amanda and I prefer to say goodbye the night before she leaves, in an intimate, stress-free environment. For example, we will usually go out for dinner and then come back home and hold each other by the fireplace before saying goodbye. The next day, she usually gets a ride to the airport from her parents instead of from me. Call me unfeeling, but I prefer to say goodbye to her alone, in front of a fireplace in the evening, than at 6:30 a.m. in a public airport, among other couples who are crying while a loud speaker announces the time when they must leave each other again. Unlike my first long-distance relationship, I now associate saying goodbye with intimate, loving evenings, instead of crying at airports and feeling miserable. What a wonderful feeling!

Losing Romantic Feelings for Your Partner

No matter how much I love Amanda, at times I find it difficult to feel romantic toward her when we are apart. This usually occurs after I haven't seen her for eight or nine weeks. I begin to feel numb and detached from any romantic feelings. I think this is a result of being alone for such a long time. By neglecting these feelings, they just seem to give up and stop asking for satisfaction altogether. My mind says I love Amanda and I want to be in a relationship. Still my feelings for romance suffer because I have not seen or touched her in such a long time.

I accept these feelings as a natural part of a long-distance relationship. I also realize that left unchecked, they could cause trouble. I have seen other couples experience feelings of indifference after being apart for several months, but instead of taking steps to remedy the problem, they began doubting the relationship and seeing other people.

This is not what I call a good ending to any relationship.

The first thing I do when I am feeling unromantic is call Amanda on the phone and tell her how much I love her. This immediately puts me back into the right emotional state and reminds me how deeply I feel for her. If my feelings of unromanticism are really strong, I will be honest with Amanda about my feelings. Confiding in her makes me feel better and eventually leads us to reassure each other that our desire to be together has not faded, but is stronger.

Sometimes all it takes to feel romantic again is to talk dirty on the phone. Why not? If you cannot see your partner, you may as well talk about what you are going to do when you will see them. Although you risk being frustrated for the evening, I have found naughty conversations to be fun and helpful in curing those long-distance blues. If nothing else, talking intimately with each other brings back memories that immediately make me feel passionate, loving, and perfectly clear on why it is worth being apart from my girlfriend for a little longer.

Another way I can bring out romantic feelings for Amanda is by sending her a really long love letter. Although not as satisfying as a conversation, I have found expressing myself in a letter to be an excellent way to rekindle romantic feelings. All I have to do is start writing about how beautiful she is, or how fortunate I feel to have her in my life, and immediately I feel like I do when she is beside me.

Unfortunately, I have not sent Amanda as many letters as I should. In fact, when she reads the above paragraph, her response will probably be, "Letters . . . what letters?" Okay, I admit I have thought about writing her love letters more than actually writing them. Still, it's the thought that counts right? Wrong. Which is why, to make up for my delinquent letter writing, I use frequent flower deliveries. Whenever I am feeling down, I pick up the phone and send Amanda some flowers with a note saying I love her or that I am thinking about her. This is only the start of feeling better. When I send her flowers during the day, I can always expect a call from her that evening, thanking me and telling me how beautiful they are. Instantly her call makes me feel wonderful (and relieves my guilt for not sending her a letter).

If I'm feeling a little down, I can always rely on my family or friends to remind me of how beautiful Amanda is and how insensitive I am. All it takes is a self-deprecating comment from me such as, "Why am I even in this relationship . . . after all, I hardly ever see Amanda," and my family is quick to remind me that I am wallowing in self-pity and should smarten up. I think they call it "tough love." A great example of what I am talking about is a typical dinner at my family's house after Amanda has been away for four or five weeks. I will start feeling sorry for myself and I will test their sympathy by asking them whether being in a long-distance relationship is worth the pain and loneliness. They, of course, will not take the bait, but comment that I should feel lucky that such a wonderful woman stays in a relationship with me at all, never mind a long-distance relationship. I always like that one, and can always count on them for an immediate pick-me-up whenever I am feeling sorry for myself.

If your family or friends support your relationship, you can find no better source to put things in perspective if you feel down. If your family and friends are like mine, they will sense when you are really down or just fishing for sympathy, and put you right back on track. I remember many times when I was really upset, and my family reminded me about how my relationship was worth the distance. Or how nothing good in life comes without sacrifices. Or how fortunate I am to have found somebody that I can love, period. Without a doubt, talking to my family and friends is one of the most powerful ways I use to maintain a passion for my relationship.

Despite anything I can do alone, the best way to feel romantic about Amanda is to be romantic with her, and I cannot do that by myself. Therefore, I try to see her every four weeks, although things do not always work out that way.

Take our last conversation for example. Before Amanda left about a month ago, we pledged that we would not go beyond four weeks without seeing each other again. When is she coming back into town? In about five or six weeks. Why? We both agreed that we have tons of work to finish and that spending a weekend with each other is not possible. Is this good for a long-distance relationship? No. Does it happen? Yes. It is funny, but no matter how hard we try, we cannot seem to avoid the "nine-week trap" in which we go for more than two months without seeing each other. No matter how much we miss one another, we get caught-up in our work and before we realize it, eight or nine weeks have passed.

When possible, I try to see Amanda at least every four weeks. I use four weeks as the limit because I find that if I stay apart from her longer than that, getting reacquainted when we finally do meet is a lot harder and takes longer. Frustrations beyond not feeling romantic also occur around the four or five-week mark. Again, a phenomenon that is best left to the imagination. Anyone who has ever been away from their partner for a month or more knows exactly what I am talking about.

For me, four is the magic number. It represents the maximum number of weeks that I can be away from Amanda without feeling unromantic. I can blame not seeing her on being too expensive, or on my job, or on her school, but if I let the time between us go beyond four weeks I really have only myself to blame. No matter how many flowers I send or how often I talk to my family, nothing I do comes close to the feeling of being with her. I think it's time to book a plane ticket.

Phone Conversations

My second long-distance relationship was fraught with phone arguments. At least once a week I found myself in a disagreement on the phone with my girlfriend. Despite my intent to keep our conversations short and happy, they always seemed to drift into long, intense discussions about personal values, politics, and whether either of us could stand being lonely any longer. We would start with talking about what we both had done during the week. At the time, we were in university, so naturally our conversation would focus on our courses and what we were learning. I don't know how it happened, but we always seemed to compare courses that taught opposing politics. For example, I would talk about a business course's perspective of the free market, then she would respond with her readings on socialism from one of her philosophy courses.

As you might have guessed, our discussions usually degenerated to a point where it was world capitalism versus Marxism. Although we both intended to talk objectively about the ideas we were experiencing, somehow we always managed to take sides and duke it out over the phone. What's worse, our arguments became personal. Soon we were not just exploring ideas, but my girlfriend actually became a radical socialist in my eyes and I, a conservative capitalist in hers. To try to win, both of us took an extreme stance. She would be advocating a fundamental economic change in the world, and I was turning back the economic clock to the 1800's!

Eventually, we would both stop arguing and start to ask frightening questions about the foundation of our relationship. Given our opposing politics, how did we ever come together? Do we really have anything in common? How can we ever hope to stay together if we cannot agree on anything? Would either of us want to live with someone so different? Maybe ending things now would be better, and we should start looking for partners with similar values. We kept asking these questions until she was in tears, I was mad, and we both became disillusioned with the future of our relationship.

Those conversations make up some of the saddest memories of my second long-distance relationship. To make matters worse, I know I could have done some simple things to avoid many of them. It is true that I did not share many of the same values as my girlfriend, but never to the degree voiced in our conversations. When we finally talked face to face, we found we had many things in common, a conclusion we could never reach after our phone arguments. On the phone we let our feelings of loneliness and insecurity come out in our belief systems, and we never knew when enough was enough in a conversation.

In retrospect, I can see now that our disagreements resulted from both of us being lonely and finding no other way to express our frustration but through self-created conflict. If we only put our loneliness aside and kept our conversations brief and focused on when we would be together next, we could have avoided many long, unhappy phone ordeals that hurt our relationship.

If you have been together with someone for more than a few months, you probably know what issues upset your partner. Different issues upset different couples. For many, talking about religion can ruin a conversation. For others, talking about casual dates with members of the opposite sex might cause an argument. Certain topics, which when discussed in person or on the phone, bother all couples. I try to identify these areas as quickly as possible by mentally taking note of them when they crop up in conversations with Amanda. As a result, I have a mental list of the topics that really bother her or me.

Given that I know what makes for a bad conversation, I try to change the subject every time an inflammatory issue arises. For example, I know that discussing politics bothers us, so when it comes up in a discussion, I change the subject to events that occurred in our lives during the week. If that topic bothers us, I will talk about the weather or social events occurring in our respective cities.

I do not try to make our conversations bland and lifeless. When I feel the odd argument brewing, I do try to change the focus to something less explosive. Discussing major issues over the phone has the tendency to be blown out of proportion and to become personal, because separating a real issue from how much I miss Amanda, is almost impossible. Also, on the phone, I can't see her facial expressions and body movements, which often tell me how she is really feeling versus how she says she is feeling. Knowing the down-side of pushing each other's wrong buttons on the phone, I try to avoid those buttons at all costs, keeping our conversation focused on something that makes us both happy.

Everyone who is in a long-distance relationship feels lonely from time to time. It goes with the territory. I feel the key is not to let loneliness rob me of the few times when I do get to talk to Amanda on the phone. If I know that I will be talking to her tonight, I try to look forward to that call and what I will say. I plan to talk about my family, health, work, or anything that is special to me and that I want to share with her. By the time she calls, I have lots of things to discuss, leaving me no time to brood about being lonely or how much I miss her.

I have found a good topic to discuss is when we will be together again. Planning our next visit helps us avoid talking about loneliness and gives us something to look forward to in the future. Talking about our next meeting inspires both of us, puts pleasant images in our minds, and makes us feel secure knowing that the loneliness we feel for each other will only be temporary. Now, when I feel myself slipping from "I really miss you, honey" to "I can't stand this loneliness anymore," I change the subject to what I want to do the next time we are together. Immediately this makes me feel happy and puts our conversation back on track.

If I do nothing else with my phone conversations, I try to keep them brief and information-based. I find that talking to Amanda for ten or fifteen minutes, four or five times a week, is better than talking to her for thirty or forty minutes, twice a week. Having shorter, more frequent conversations allows us to speak with each other every day. We can tell one another what happened while it is still fresh in our minds. This eliminates the possibility of forgetting details if we had to wait until the end of the week. Speaking frequently also makes us feel closer because we know everything the other person is doing and feeling daily. Talking to each other at the end of a long day lifts our spirits, and gives us something to look forward to tomorrow.

Another major benefit of having short, frequent conversations is that they force us to keep our talks light and information-based. In fifteen or twenty minutes, all we have time to do is tell each other what we did during the day and that we love each other, the end. We don't have time to feel lonely, get into an argument, or analyse issues in our relationship to a point where we find no other alternative but separation.

I want to stress again that I do not try to remove everything with meaning from my phone conversations. However, I do defer discussing major issues in our relationship until I am face to face with Amanda, or until the time when I can see her facial expressions and interpret her body language. You can easily say "it's over" and hang up the phone on someone. After all, a phone is merely a voice attached to a lifeless instrument that one can turn off and on at will. However, when I am face to face with her it is a lot harder just to unplug the relationship. If I need to discuss something important with her immediately, I do so. If the discussion starts leading to an argument or to the questioning of our relationship, I try to defer it until we can be together. When I cannot wait until our next planned visit, I get on a plane and go to Amanda or vice versa. If the issue is that important, the least I can do is give both of us the chance to decide after discussing things in person.

I try to interpret verbal cues accurately on the phone. For example, last week we were talking and based on the withdrawn tone in Amanda's voice, I thought that she was upset with me. At the end of the conversation, I asked her if she was annoyed and she said "no," but she had developed a sore throat during the day and was not feeling well. If I had not asked and she had not thought of telling me that she was sick (because she would not want me to worry), I would have left the conversation thinking she was mad at me. This in turn would have lead to an unpleasant evening with me brooding over something that in reality, was the farthest thing from the truth.

Now whenever I sense that Amanda is giving me negative verbal cues on the phone, I don't make any rash interpretations. Instead, I tell her how I feel and ask her to explain herself. If her response doesn't feel right, I ask her again. In fact, I keep asking until I know the reason why I am feeling uncomfortable with her tone or rhythm. Periodically I may uncover something unsettling behind her cues. Although unpleasant, I would find this out in time anyway. If I do not ask her to clarify her signals, however, I risk leaving the conversation uncertain whether something is upsetting her or not. I don't know about you, but I do not like being upset for no reason, so I find it's worth the effort to determine what Amanda is really feeling before I put down the phone. It not only eases my mind, but shows I care.

Being Tempted to Give Up on Your Relationship

Every relationship has its problems, and long-distance relationships are no exception. I feel like giving up sometimes, and I know Amanda does too. If you haven't seen your partner for months, your mind starts playing tricks on you, it's only natural. Maybe it's a friend who tells you that your relationship is too stressful and that you would be better off without it. You might be at a family dinner where everyone agrees it would be easier if you dated someone closer to home. What about an attractive person in a night club who comes up to you and asks you to come back to their house for the evening?

Every day I could find a thousand reasons to leave Amanda, and they might not even involve the need to date other people. Simply sitting alone in a room and thinking about how my relationship will not work, is a very effective way to start destroying it. I could start asking myself why should I make sacrifices for someone that I hardly ever see? How much longer can I endure being apart from Amanda? Even if I do persevere, what if she finally decides not to return?

Driving yourself into a mental frenzy that eventually will sour your feelings toward your partner, is not hard. By asking the right questions, you can easily convince yourself why you must leave them immediately. Without even seeing your partner, you can lead yourself to believe that your relationship is destined to fail. In actuality this may be the furthest from the truth, but that will not matter once you fall into a thought-rut. I have observed it repeatedly. Things are going great in a friend's relationship, then one day their partner talks to the wrong person or starts asking themselves the wrong questions, and they start doubting the relationship. A doubting partner is painful in any relationship, but especially so in one where you cannot be near them to defend yourself.

Whether it's another person's advances in a night club, or just a lonely Saturday night in which you think yourself into a fit, the only way to combat temptations is to commit to your relationship 100%. Problems will arise, but if you are really committed, nothing should sway you.

I constantly endure periods of doubt and temptation, some more successfully than others. I have felt angry, deprived, and trapped. I have felt like I was missing things in life. I also have felt like I just didn't have the energy to continue loving Amanda. So what got me through? Commitment. No matter how bad I felt, I always returned to feeling 100% committed to my relationship and to the love I feel for Amanda---a powerful force. So powerful, in fact, that it alone pulls me back to where I should be every time I feel really detached.

Although committing to your relationship is essential to staying in it, you can do some practical things to avoid thought-ruts. The first is ignoring support systems that you know may not approve of your partner, especially when you are feeling down or lonely. If you know that a friend or a family member may disapprove, do not go and talk to them when you feel like leaving. Without a doubt, my family and friends lend strength to my relationship by supporting it. They are the people I trust and respect most, which makes their approval a powerful confirmation that I am doing the right thing by staying involved with Amanda. If they did not approve of her, however, it would make it a lot harder to justify staying with her, especially during times when I doubt our relationship myself.

I am not saying to avoid your family and friends. In fact, if most of the people who know you disapprove of your relationship, you may have a real problem. That was the case in my last romance, one, which as my family predicted, was destined for failure because I had completely incompatible values with my girlfriend. If you do know of any obvious critics, and we all have them, just avoid talking to them about your relationship. The drawback is that you can't discuss everything you may want with these people, but the benefit is avoiding a conversation that might pollute your mind with doubts that aren't justified.

I like to have a good time, like most people. Socializing and meeting new people are fun pastimes. If I have not seen Amanda for several weeks, and I choose to go out with friends, I must accept certain realities. One is that I will probably meet women who feel just as lonely. The second, is that on a crowded dance floor at 1 a.m., a 100% commitment to my relationship may not be the first thing on my mind. This does not mean that anything will happen, but putting myself in that situation, increases the likelihood of it occurring. I am not going to hibernate in my home while Amanda is at university. Life's too short for that. Nevertheless, when I do go out, especially when I am feeling a little deprived, I try to be aware of the temptations that exist in certain situations. No one is perfect, including myself, but if I want to stay in a trusting, committed, loving relationship--and I do--it helps to avoid situations that make it easy to compromise myself.

If my mind wanders too far into doubt, it always helps to think about why I wanted to be in a relationship in the first place. One reason was that I loved Amanda very much and felt I could trust her completely. Another reason was our similar values and respect for our families. I felt we could both complement and support each other in whatever the other person wanted to do in life. Thinking about these reasons works wonders for me. If I am down or doubting whether I have enough energy to continue, I just have to think about why I got involved in our relationship in the first place, and suddenly I feel like I did when I first started falling in love with Amanda. This is not a substitute for seeing her in person, but it is a good way to chase away those self-created thought monsters that creep up on me from time to time.

If I cannot resolve things on my own, I try to talk to Amanda about my feelings before they get out of control. This is not always a pleasant experience. No partner wants to hear that you are doubting the relationship, especially when they are not. It's hard not to take it personally when someone you love, phones you and tells you that they are "reassessing their commitment," or "rethinking our future together." You feel slighted, angry, and hurt, all at once. Honesty is painful sometimes. Yet I think the alternative is worse. If you don't talk about doubting feelings, they will eat away at you until you can no longer bear it and you must leave your relationship. If I tell Amanda that I am having doubts, at least she has an immediate chance to assure me that my fears are unfounded. Yet if I don't tell her about my uncertainty, I might continue to doubt forever. In fact, I believe that if I didn't express certain feelings to her in the past, they probably would have destroyed our relationship. For months, I would have convinced myself that we were doomed, and by the time Amanda might have guessed what I was feeling, she would not have been able to say anything to make things right. It's sad to think that if people were honest about their feelings with their partner a little earlier, they might have saved their relationship.

Emotional Stages in a Long-Distance Relationship

Whenever Amanda leaves town, I go through the same emotional stages. It's unavoidable. In the first couple of weeks I feel happy and free. It's unfortunate that she is leaving town, but I know it's for the best. I accept that I will be without her for several weeks and try to think positively. It feels good that I can focus exclusively on my work, and wonder what I am going to do with all my free time.

By week three, my feelings of happiness and freedom turn to loneliness. I begin to feel I have too much free time, time that could be spent with Amanda. I really start to miss her. I also begin asking myself those evil "Why?" questions. Questions like, "Why can't she be in town?" or "Why didn't I book a plane ticket to see her?" or "Why couldn't we live in cities that are driving-distance apart?"

By the fourth or fifth week, I convince myself that I won't be seeing Amanda anytime soon and that there is nothing I can do about it. This realization makes me frustrated and upset. The "Why" questions that searched for a solution now turn into no-win statements that only serve to make me more agitated. Instead of asking myself, "Why didn't I book a plane ticket?" I ask, "Why do I have to endure this suffering week after week?" or "Why can't I be in a normal relationship?" or "Why do I keep putting myself in these situations?"

Around the seventh or eighth week, I stop being upset and start becoming detached. I wake up in the morning and wonder whether I'm in a relationship at all. I ask myself what it is like to kiss Amanda and start questioning whether her physical appearance has changed. However, unlike the "Why" questions, these thoughts do not evoke any emotion. The best way I can describe my feelings around week eight or nine is a tired numbness. My mind and body have gone through so many draining emotions that they just decide to give up. I know that I still love Amanda, but I can't feel anything else.

The emotional roller-coaster that I just described shocked me in my first two relationships. In fact, I felt like I was losing my mind. Who could have guessed that I would experience such a range of emotions in such a short period of time. I thought I was going to stay in the happy and free stage forever. Little did I know that a few weeks later, I would wonder whether I was even in a relationship.

Now that I am in my third long-distance romance, I accept two things. One is that emotional stages are inevitable. I thought they were unique to my first relationship, but they were not. The second is that I do not have to lose my mind if I am aware of what emotional stage I am in, and cope with it accordingly. Of course, things are never that simple when I am dealing with emotions, especially my own. The alternative is to avoid my feelings, and hope by the time I feel indifferent, I do not react negatively and accidentally end my relationship.

All I can say about the first two weeks of being away from someone you love, is to enjoy it while it lasts. Every time Amanda leaves town, I promise myself this time is going to be different. I promise myself that I will be happy with working, exercising, reading, visiting my family, and talking to her on the phone. I know I won't see her for months, but in my mind that isn't so bad, because we both agreed that it was best that we were apart temporarily to do what makes both of us feel happy in life.

As it turns out, I usually am happy for the first couple of weeks. No problem. The difficulty lies in prolonging these feelings. No matter how hard I try, I cannot make them last beyond three or four weeks. I guess it isn't that bad, compared to my last relationship when I was devastated the minute my girlfriend left town. If I had my wish, I would be happy all the time, no matter how long Amanda is away. Therefore, whenever she leaves town, I try to think back to the first couple of weeks without her and I recall those same emotions. Does it work? Sometimes, but it gets more difficult as time passes. Will I keep trying? Of course. If I just keep stretching those memories a little further, one day Amanda will be back permanently and it will be like she never left town.

♡♡♡

Around the third or fourth week, I start feeling lonely and sorry for myself. I see other couples out together, and no matter how hard I try, I can't help but to miss her. I try not to suppress these feelings because I feel they are a natural part of being apart from anyone, especially a loved one. After all, I entered into a relationship with Amanda because I wanted to spend more time with her, not less. If I did not feel lonely, something would be wrong.

What I do try to do is avoid asking myself useless questions like, "Why can't I see Amanda?" Instead, I ask, "How can I book a ticket to see her in a couple of weeks?" Of course hopping a plane every time you are lonely is not always possible. Planes aren't free. You also can't just leave your work or studies when you feel like it. Whatever the reason, it is not the answer to the question that is important, but the question itself. Rather than using questions to put myself into no-win situations, I try to use them to look for solutions. I still feel lonely now and again, but at least my mind stays preoccupied with how to make myself feel better rather than just wondering why I feel so alone. If you doubt the power of good questions, just think about this book. It represents the answer to my question, "What can I do on weekends to stay happy while Amanda is out of town?"

I can relate to being upset and frustrated, because it is the feeling that I am experiencing right now in my relationship. Amanda has been out of town for about a month. I have gone past the stage of being lonely, and now feel angry that I cannot see her for another four weeks. I knew she was going to be gone for two months, but it doesn't seem to matter. Whenever I talk to her on the phone, I can't avoid asking when she is coming home, like a kid in the car blurting out, "Are we there yet," every ten minutes of the ride. I know exactly the date when she is returning. Still, I cannot resist questioning her repeatedly to reinforce in my mind that she is not coming back for a month and there's nothing I can do about it.

This is not healthy, but I am only human. After a month, I can't help but be angry and frustrated because I really miss her. I do have options, however. I can let these feelings consume me, or I can channel them into something productive.

Although it is one of the most difficult things in life, I am trying not to let my feelings run away on me. It is not easy, but I am willing to try because I feel my relationship is worth it. Asking good questions helps, writing helps, talking to family and friends helps, and confiding in Amanda helps. What can I say? Anyone who has been in any relationship knows they take work. Dealing with anger and frustration when your partner leaves town is no exception to the rule.

Feeling detached is one of the scariest and most dangerous feelings I have experienced in my relationship. I say it is scary, because after being apart for eight or nine weeks, some days I wake up in the morning and wonder whether I'm in a relationship. I still love Amanda, but it has been so long since I've seen her that I begin to lose the feeling of being with her. It's the most difficult experience to describe. All I can say is that it is frightening the first couple of times you go through it. The first time I felt detached in a relationship I thought I stopped loving my girlfriend. That wasn't true, I just hadn't been near her in a long time. I was committed to her, however, so instead of doing something rash, I waited until I saw her again. When I finally did, I had no doubt in my mind that I still loved her and everything was fine.

If I concluded that I didn't love my girlfriend anymore, I might have ended the relationship. This is why I consider the detachment stage dangerous. Detachment is an emotion that creeps up on you unexpectedly. If you're not aware that you are feeling detached, you may interpret it as the end, when it may only be the result of not seeing your partner for such a long time. If I feel detached, it probably means that Amanda will be coming home soon, so I accept it and try to ignore it until she gets home. The good thing about detachment is that when you finally do get together with your loved one, you should have a great time becoming reattached.

I'll be straight with you. I hate going through the emotional stages of a long-distance relationship. I also realize that I can't do anything about it in the future. So if I still want to be in my relationship-- and I do--I am going to have to persevere. I will do and say things I know are wrong. I will feel emotions that I do not like, but what's the alternative? To anyone who is committed to a long-distance relationship, do not give up hope. If it's any comfort, know that people like you everywhere are going through the same thing and loving/hating every moment of it.

Growing While Apart and Getting Reacquainted

If I have learnt one thing from long-distance relationships, it's that no matter how much you love someone, you can't avoid growing apart from that person if you are away from them for any length of time. Every time Amanda leaves the city, we grow in different ways apart from one another. It makes sense when you think about it. After all, when we leave each other, we don't stop growing as people, but because we cannot share the same experiences, we cannot help growing in different directions. I live in the middle of the country, work in business, and socialize mainly with older acquaintances. She, on the other hand, lives on the east coast, goes to university, and socializes with younger students. Whereas my life and friends usually revolve around business, Amanda is focused on academics and accustomed to a collegiate lifestyle.

The point I am making, is that given our different physical locations, interests, and experiences, we can't help but grow when we're away from each other. We update each other on the phone and by mail, but it's different from talking face to face. If one of us goes through a meaningful experience, the other person cannot truly appreciate it until we get together, and by that time it is usually too late. We try hard to keep each other abreast of our experiences and feelings, but we cannot share everything like we could if we were together.

I do not find growing while apart from Amanda to be destructive. It is something that I have grown to accept as a natural part of being in a long-distance romance. In fact, I find that growing while apart makes things more interesting. After all, I don't know many other couples that can share experiences from diverse cities, occupations, and circles of friends in every conversation.

Growing in separate directions is easy. Getting reacquainted is another story. When we finally get together, I can't escape feelings of anxiety and unfamiliarity similar to the ones that I felt on our first date. Why? I think it relates to the fact that in many ways, Amanda is never the same person I kissed goodbye the last time we saw each other. Besides the fact that she physically changes (although slightly) in six to eight weeks, I find that her perspectives change. I expect her to have the same opinion on issues, when in actuality she may have changed her opinions based on experiences that I never even knew she had. This frequently shocks me, leaving me with the feeling that she has changed overnight and that I don't know her anymore. Of course her views did not change that quickly and are explainable by her experiences. Still, I never know that, and can only compare her to when I last saw her, which may have been several months ago.

The reacquaintment process does not stop there. Accompanying the feelings of anxiety and unfamiliarity are usually disagreements over issues such as politics and religion, or roles in relationships, or my favourite, disagreements about each other's idiosyncrasies. It's funny, but when Amanda leaves the city, I only think about her good qualities and forget her shortcomings. I know she does the same, because every time we get together, we discover our shortcomings all over again. I may suddenly feel that she wants to socialize too much with friends or she may think that I don't socialize enough. We knew this about each other when we committed to going out and accepted the difference. Yet when we are apart, we easily forget these differences, leading to a rude awakening when we finally reunite.

I've found that the best way to deal with the reacquaintment process is to be aware that it is coming, and to separate real issues from the negative effects of the process itself.

Don't fool yourself into thinking that you won't have to become reacquainted with your partner the next time you see them. It never works out that way. I am writing this paragraph a day after a disagreement that I know was associated with the reacquaintment process. She has been in town for only three weeks, is leaving in two days, and we just discovered that I don't take an interest in her friends as much as she would like. I admit to this, because when she is in town for only three weeks, I am more interested in spending time with her. Exclusively. Anyway, this lead to a disagreement and some hurt feelings yesterday evening. However, while driving home, I realized that it wasn't such a big issue after all, and that many of her feelings probably had resulted from getting reacquainted with me. As it turns out, I did agree to take more of an interest in her friends when she is in town for longer than a month, but I wasn't as hurt as I could have been if I didn't know what was going on. Although my interest in her friends is a real issue, I realized that she was more sensitive to this because she had grown unaccustomed to my habits while she was away at university. This realization allowed me to discuss the issue without blowing things out of proportion, despite how intense Amanda's emotions were at the time.

If you don't understand where your partner is coming from, find out by asking lots of questions. If Amanda says something out of the blue that shocks me, instead of getting upset, I try to find out if something has happened in her life that I was unaware of to cause her to think that way. A good example of this was a disagreement that we had on her last visit. Over dinner, we began a conversation about how biology may play a role in people's behaviour. Well, what started as a harmless topic (or so I thought) turned into heated debate over whether we should excuse criminals from their crimes based on biological grounds. Amanda maintained that we should not excuse them on any grounds. However, I felt like playing the devil's advocate that evening. I maintained that given breakthroughs in genetic research, we may excuse criminals based on biological defects in the future.

This conversation may sound ridiculous to you, but no one planned for it to happen . . . I promise you. It was just one of those wayward discussions where before I knew what was going on, Amanda was storming away from the table in tears, thinking I was cruel and unfeeling.

If we left the evening at that, the results may have been devastating. Instead, after we both settled down, I started asking her questions about her studies at university. What resulted was my realization that she had been studying and discussing this issue intensely over the past year and had formulated some very passionate opinions about it. After questioning me, she realized that I was simply playing devil's advocate and was treating the issue lightly because I hadn't thought about it as much as she had, nor had I formulated such strong opinions. By asking questions calmly and rationally, we discovered where we were both coming from, which made both of us feel a lot better. Instead of damaging our relationship, I became more sensitive to how strongly she felt about the issue. She realized that I needed more time to sort out my feelings.

If disagreements do get personal, I ask Amanda for specific explanations and examples so the discussion doesn't become hurtful. In our disagreement about my lack of interest in her friends, I asked for specific examples of when I was insensitive to them. She in turn responded with several instances where I could have joined in more. Yet she did admit that I wasn't always insensitive. In fact, she gave almost as many examples of when I was sensitive to her friends as when I was not.

Asking for specific examples did two things. First, it changed Amanda's criticism of me from my being insensitive all of the time, to my being insensitive occasionally. This made me feel a lot less hurt, and gave me hope in the conversation, knowing that at least I was responsive to her friends some of the time. The second thing that specific examples did was to clarify when I was interested in her friends and when I was not. By the end of our conversation, I knew exactly how to be more caring and could commit to improving. After all, if I had done it several times in the past, all I had to do was remember what I did then and repeat that in the future.

Pointing out problems is fine, but finding solutions and compromising is the important thing. Otherwise, our relationship will never improve.

Again, and for the last time, I refer to "The Great Insensitivity Debate," or my so-called uncaring attitude towards Amanda's friends. She is going to love reading this. "Everyone will hate me after they read this," she will say. To balance the scales, therefore, just let me say that despite our disagreements, she is the most beautiful, optimistic, honest, and caring woman I have ever met. I love her very much.

As you might have guessed, our discussion ended with a joint solution in which we both compromised. I agreed to be more sensitive to her friends, and she agreed that she would reduce the number of group events that she expected to be at when she was in town, especially when she was here for only a few weeks. Why did this solution feel so satisfying? Because we came to it together. More important, it represented compromise that respected both of our feelings. No one won the disagreement. Both of us learnt more about the other, and came to an agreement that hopefully will strengthen our relationship and reduce similar misunderstandings in the future.

Try to keep things in perspective and realize that you can solve only so many issues until you are together permanently. I have to keep reminding myself that time and togetherness are the only remedies for most problems. I also find that before I know it, Amanda has to leave town, and I realize that we have spent lots of time struggling with issues that we couldn't possibly have solved in such a short visit. I promise myself repeatedly that the next time I feel an impossible issue brewing, I will just stop talking and kiss her rather than wasting time dealing with challenges that may require a lifetime together to solve.

The last quality of the reacquaintment process that I have come to appreciate is that you never have enough time to go through it properly. When Amanda returns, she has to spend time with her mother, her father, and her brother. She also has to spend time with her friends. In fact, if she did not value our time together and was unable to manage the constant guilt trips family and friends usually place on her, we probably wouldn't see each other at all. I have found that she has many demands on her time, and if we wanted to, we could find some excuse to avoid the reacquaintment process entirely. For us, the key is that we are aware that our time together is limited, and yet we try to see each other even if it means having to endure some getting-to-know-you pains. Like everything in a relationship, planning time together requires effort on both of our parts. Nevertheless, if we both try, we can spend quality time together at no expense to either of our family or friends.

Communicating

I t's a constant struggle to keep close to your loved one in a long-distance relationship without going bankrupt. I can't see Amanda, so naturally I want to talk to her more. Unfortunately, if I phoned her every time I wanted to talk, I would have to work for the phone company full time just to pay off my long-distance debts. It is probably just as well, because if I could afford all the calls I wanted to make, I would call her constantly and both of us would never get any work done. Happily, I have found a balance between staying in touch and not completely emptying my bank account. The balance, however, demands that we both be flexible and creative in how we communicate. Where does this flexibility and creativity stem from? It comes from the sick feeling I have immediately after I read my long-distance phone bill detailing all the prime time calls I made in the first month after Amanda left town.

If you are not on a long-distance phone plan, get on one immediately! It doesn't matter whether it's offered by Sprint, MCI, AT&T, Unitel, or some other phone company. Find the plan that offers the best rates to where you are calling to, and sign up. You will thank yourself after receiving your next phone bill. Of course, the best way to reduce costs is to make long-distance calls in off hours, or not make them at all. Practically, when I need to talk to Amanda, I could care less what time it was, and even less about whether I should be making the call at all. After three or four weeks of being apart, am I not entitled to call her when I want? Of course I am. It's just this type of thinking that demands a calling plan.

Although not as satisfying as a phone conversation, leaving a message on an answering machine is a good, inexpensive way to keep in touch during the day. I enjoy nothing more than coming home from work to find Amanda's voice on my answering machine, asking me how my day went. Ok, I enjoy one thing more, having her ask me in person. Given that I can't see Amanda whenever I want, I don't want to miss anytime that she wants to communicate with me. Talking by way of our answering machines is better than no communication

at all. Even if I just want to say, "Hi . . . I love you
. . . I will call later," leaving a message is an
important way to stay in touch with her anytime of
the day. I warn you, however, answering machines
break down. When they do, be prepared to face the
anxiety of someone who desperately needed to talk
to you all day but found no response on your
answering machine.

I use lots of nonverbal ways to stay in touch
with Amanda. One way I like best is sending
flowers. Every few weeks, I will call the same
florist (it's good to train them so you do not have to
waste much time on the phone) and have a different
assortment of freshly, cut flowers delivered to her
with a note saying "I love you" or "Thinking of
you." This may not be the most original gift, but
she really loves flowers, and no matter how often I
send them to her, she still appreciates the gesture. I
never tell her when they are coming, which always
makes them a surprise and extra special. Amanda
also sends me gifts such as books or music. She has
even sent flowers to my office a couple of times,

something that my male co-workers make sure never to let me forget.

No one can deny it, we are in the information age, and one of the best tools to communicate rapidly is the fax machine. Amanda is the best at using the fax. Out of the blue she will write me a one page love letter and fax it to my office. I thought the flower jokes at the office were bad until I started getting reactions from co-workers on my love faxes. Frequent faxes have seemed to help the situation, and now Amanda's faxes are commonplace at the office (the secretary only reads them to herself instead of to the whole office).

I have used electronic mail (E-mail) often in the past to stay in touch with a girlfriend. My first long-distance relationship is an example of this phenomenon. Humorously, it was not only a long-distance relationship, but a long-distance courtship as well. It began after I finished a summer educational program focusing on entrepreneurship and technology in my hometown. Students from all over the country were flown in for an intensive four week program requiring all participants to live, eat, and learn together in a university residence for the duration. We established close friendships, and not a dry eye could be found on the last day of the session. Knowing the extent of the friendships made, combined with the fact that everyone was from different parts of the country, the program's administrators decided to issue E-mail accounts to all of the students. No matter where we travelled afterwards, these accounts would allow us to communicate with each other and with other students from similar programs that took place at various universities throughout the country. All you had to know was another student's E-mail account name. Using this name and a personal computer, you could speak to the person electronically, or send them electronic letters. A lonely techi's dream come true.

Several months after the program ended, I began speaking and writing electronically to a girl who attended a similar program in another city. At first, as I did with other E-mail holders on the system, I compared notes with her on our respective experiences. As months passed, however, our electronic conversations became more personal. We started talking about our families, values, and career aspirations. In time we began discussing romantic interests. Now you may begin to think that this is unusual, but don't knock it until you try it. Although E-mail may seem like an unconventional communication tool, it allows you to send and receive love letters instantaneously, with minimal time, effort, and cost, compared with the phone, mail, or fax. To a long-distance pioneer like myself, this meant I could romance a girl constantly with little expense and without ever needing to be physically by her.

Of course E-mail only goes so far. In time, we sent each other pictures of ourselves, talked on the phone, and planned a rendezvous at the end of the summer when she would fly out and stay with me for a few weeks. This was quite a gamble on our part given that we had never physically seen or been with each other before. The gamble paid off, and our two weeks together were one of the most memorable times of my life. After we got over the formalities of introductions and our shared uneasiness with our first meeting, we fell head over heels for each other, both emotionally and physically. Upon parting to different universities, we cried and pledged that we would never stop writing, talking, and visiting each other.

After two months in university, my passion seemed to dry up as fast as my tears, as did hers. We were both seeing other people, only communicating sporadically via E-mail, and had no plans of seeing each other in the future. In other words, the relationship was over, but without E-mail, I wouldn't have even been in a relationship.

Today I do not use E-mail to talk to my current girlfriend, but we have discussed getting accounts in the next year on the global information network called the Internet. If you are unfamiliar with E-mail, you can find lots of books in the library that will tell you about the most popular networks (e.g., Internet, Compuserve, America Online, Prodigy), how to get an account, and how to use it properly without offending other users. You would be surprised at the formality that you must use on an E-mail network to avoid being called a rude amateur--- never mind a rude amateur who desperately needs to talk to his girlfriend.

I don't write many letters, but when I do, I have found writing (especially a love letter) to be one of the most passionate and sincere ways of communicating with Amanda. I find something about a handwritten letter that faxes or E-mail can never duplicate. Letters from Amanda are incredibly personal because they are her thoughts in her handwriting. Her letters also tell me that she has taken the time to think about and write down her feelings on paper--a very personal gesture. Now I'm feeling guilty. I think I'm going to write to her tonight.

The last way I try to be closer to Amanda is through frequent flyer programs. My program allows me to accumulate travel miles whenever I use my credit card or take a flight with a specific airline. After banking 20,000 miles, I can redeem them for a free return ticket to anywhere in the country. Although this only results in about one ticket every year or so, it allows me to see Amanda one more time a year for free. Now I also pay my long-distance phone bills using my credit card, so the more I talk to her, the more miles I get so I can see her sooner. A dream come true. Never underestimate the ability of communication companies to take advantage of your emotions at their weakest moment.

Trusting Your Partner When They Are Away

I think trust is necessary in any relationship, but in a long-distance one it is essential. For unlike seeing your partner every day, I may not see Amanda for months. Therefore, all I have is trust to keep our relationship alive. If I needed to see and touch Amanda daily to reaffirm my trust and love for her, I probably would have given up after the first week we were apart.

I must assume certain things if I want to survive daily. The first is that Amanda loves me and is committed to us. The second is that no matter what happens while we are apart, we will both work on maintaining our love and commitment for each other. Without these assumptions, I could not get through the day. I would constantly be wondering if Amanda still loved me or if she were seeing other people. We will have our problems, but once I lose the belief that Amanda loves me, it is over. Unlike conflicting travel plans or a phone argument, trusting her love is the basis of our entire relationship.

I have found that trust has two parts. One is mental and the other is emotional. Mentally, I can tell myself I trust Amanda and that is that. I will not even think about anything else because that would be counter productive. Emotionally, however, I need to feel Amanda is acting in a way that supports my trust. Whereas the mental process is immediate, the emotional one is ongoing, in which both of us must behave in a way that reaffirms our love and trust in each other. This may be by spending time together, or simply by explaining how committed we are to each other on the phone. I cannot think of an easy way to build emotional trust. It is a long and never-ending process in which one's trust strengthens, weakens, then strengthens again. However, I have found that I can do something to help the process. At the very least, I can take steps to avoid losing trust in my relationship over a misunderstanding, or because I let my imagination get the better of me.

In my first year of university, I became acquainted with a girl who had very liberal ideas about relationships and sexuality. She believed that she could be committed to a relationship while maintaining casual sexual contact with other partners. By the second year of college, the girl was involved with a guy she met on campus. The relationship continued until one summer when she went to Germany to work. It still might have endured if he had not found out that she was sleeping with other people in Germany. The interesting thing, however, after talking to friends that knew both of them, was that she could not understand why he broke up with her when she returned to university after the summer. After all, in her mind, she was only doing what she believed to be acceptable. He, on the other hand, had expected that she would remain monogamous while in Germany. Before her leaving, both were committed to the relationship. Both were also unclear of the other's expectations, and by the time they discovered that their expectations were different, their relationship was over.

For me, the message in the above story is clear. Before committing to being in a long-distance relationship with someone, discuss your expectations with each other. This may be a healthy thing to do in any relationship, but it is essential in a long-distance one. Why? Because your partner must constantly interpret your expectations without you being physically present to represent yourself. Unlike being together all of the time, which allows you to observe your partner's behaviour and reclarify your expectations every day, a long-distance relationship offers no such luxury. Amanda must constantly guess and act on my expectations without me being there to give her my feelings about whether her guess was correct or not. Consequently, I find it crucial to stress what I expect from her, in person, to avoid either of us doing something in each other's absence that may jeopardize our love.

It's impossible to clarify all of our expectations in one visit. It is an ongoing process that we need to repeat as our needs change and our relationship grows. What's important is that we have agreed on our major expectations, such as a total committment to each another and the security to discuss problems openly as they arise. In my mind these are necessities, or understandings that we must both share if we want to stay together.

♡♡♡

After we agreed on the ground rules, I had to trust that Amanda would live up to those rules, and vice versa. Blind faith is a good term to describe this kind of trust because we cannot see each other to confirm that we are still committed to our relationship. Instead, we must rely on letters and phone conversations to reassure ourselves that we still love one another.

I think the hardest time to trust Amanda is when we first started our relationship. Both of us were committed to each other, but I was still uneasy about how she would react when we were apart. These feelings were not isolated to my current situation. In all of my past long-distance experiences, I have had to battle overwhelming feelings of distrust during the early stages of commitment, feelings that my girlfriend may be seeing someone else, or feelings that she might be falling out of love with me because she could not see or be with me. Yet always, I was able to get over these suspicions as I talked to Amanda and began to realize that she was doing nothing more than feeling lonely and waiting by the phone to hear my voice again.

I have found no easy prescription for building trust in the early stages of a relationship. It is an incremental, emotional process in which someone consistently meets your expectations and vice versa. I find a good way to build trust is to remember the golden rule: do unto others as you would have them do unto you. If I love Amanda so much that the very thought of cheating on her is absurd, then wouldn't she be feeling the same way? Whenever I think Amanda is cheating on me, I just think about the consequences of cheating on her. The resulting feelings are so disturbing, that my mind cannot fathom how she could decide to do the same.

No matter how much you trust someone, everyone feels insecure at some time in their relationship. When I do, I communicate my fears to Amanda openly and honestly. Simply telling her that I feel insecure makes me feel better immediately. I have the satisfaction that she knows what I am going through and understands my feelings. Often she admits to feeling the same way, which makes us realize that we are in the same situation and can work together to meet a common challenge. Also, voicing my insecurities and having Amanda assure me that she is living up to my expectations, eliminates many problems that my imagination can cause if I am doubting her commitment. If I feel insecure and do not alleviate my insecurity, my mind will dwell on that and eventually distort reality to a point where it doesn't matter whether my uncertainty was justified or not. I have seen too many friends stop communicating and destroy their relationship because they thought that their partner stopped loving them without even asking them if it was true.

The one thing that there is an abundance of in my relationship is time, time to plan when I will see Amanda again, time to sit by the phone and wait for it to ring, and time to think about her falling out of love with me. In fact, I have found that if one hopes to survive a long-distance relationship, you must learn to keep busy and focus on things other than your relationship when your partner is away. When Amanda leaves town, besides my work, I exercise, read, write, visit my family, and listen to music. If I spent all my time thinking about my relationship and what Amanda was doing, I would start feeling insecure. This is especially true when I round the eighth or ninth week away from her. I find it is around this time that my imagination plays tricks on me. It may suggest, for example, that my relationship is dissolving or some other absurd idea. This is when it is crucial to keep yourself occupied. I try to remember that dwelling on insecurities, in times of loneliness, will not bring Amanda to me any sooner, but may ruin my next talk or visit with her. Therefore I keep loving her in my mind and look forward to her next visit. If I feel my imagination going astray, I try to change my focus to an activity or thought completely unrelated to her and I.

While in university, going through my second long-distance romance, I had the good fortune to meet a friend who always listened to me when I needed to talk about it. He always encouraged me to stay in my relationship no matter how impossible the situation appeared to me sometimes. After having an argument on the phone with my girlfriend, I would go out to dinner with my friend. We would talk about the disagreement, and instead of encouraging my feelings of lost hope, he would reassure me that our fallout was merely a result of me being lonely. It wasn't because of conflicting values or some other major problem that I might have thought existed between us at the time. My friend always convinced me that once I was with her face to face, my loneliness would disappear and so would the many conflicts that stemmed from those feelings.

If the argument was serious, I would discuss it with a close family member, who would also reassure me that many of my feelings were a result of loneliness and not a personality conflict. They would help me to focus on loving my girlfriend and looking forward to the next time when we could be together, rather than our argument on the phone. They would assure me that being in my relationship was worthwhile, and that remaining calm was the best remedy until I could discuss important issues with her in person without feelings of loneliness clouding my perspective.

By the end of my conversations with either my friend or my family, my feelings of hopelessness and frustration were transformed to calmness, love, and security. I would have renewed faith in my relationship, assured that once I was with my girlfriend the many problems we were experiencing on the phone would disappear. If I surrounded myself with people who did not support my relationship, the results might have been very different. If after an argument, my friend or family persuaded me that the disagreement meant the end of my relationship, I would have likely stayed angry and lost hope within weeks of being apart from her.

Now I know that if I want to stay involved in a long-distance romance I must associate with people who support it. When I feel that things may be falling apart, these people will comfort me and help me change my feelings from despair to hope. I do not surround myself with people who will feed into my insecurities by recommending that I would be better off without my girlfriend. Instead, I actively seek out the advice of people who are positive, supportive, and truly aware of my desire to be happy and committed to my relationship.

Signs That a Long-Distance Relationship Is Ending

From my experience, a serious long-distance relationship has only three conclusions. You can either continue your relationship from afar, come together permanently, or break up.

Continuing for a prolonged period of time is something I can relate to because it is what I am doing right now. Although I do not like the distance in my relationship, it is something I have to accept for the next couple of years if I want to keep going out with my girlfriend. Her university is on the other side of the country and the nature of my work will not allow me to move to where she lives. If we regard each other's education and work as an important part of our relationship . . . and we do . . . there's nothing we can do about the distance.

My hope is that one day we will be together. Hope is not a strong enough word. The vision of us being together permanently is the driving force in our relationship. It is also the main reason I can go weeks without seeing her and not completely lose my mind or passion. No matter how many ways I can devise to survive being apart from her, I never lose sight of one goal: to be together.

Unlike some couples, I do not intend to devise elaborate systems of travel and communication to cope with a permanent, distant relationship. From my perspective, after so many years of being apart, one may as well say they are in a "virtual" relationship, or they are romantically involved with someone that they will rarely ever touch or see.

Of course, one always has a third option. You can break up with your partner. Although I have not faced this situation currently, I did live through a break up with my last girlfriend. Why dedicate a chapter to the experience? I think it is important because if I could have changed one thing, it would have been to realize when it was over. Instead of recognizing what I now know to be the signs that my relationship was ending, I stayed in it until things got really ugly. It reached a point where we couldn't talk on the phone without arguing about some issue that lead us to conclude our values were completely incompatible and our romance was doomed. As it turned out, we were right. We were doomed. Still, the pain and arguments lasted for months before we called it quits. This was not a pleasant experience, I can assure you. Of course if you love someone, you will likely try everything to avoid breaking up, it's natural. Nevertheless, if I ever experience the following warning signs in my current relationship, I will do my best to end it quickly, rather than prolong the suffering for months. It just wouldn't be fair to either of us.

In time, every phone conversation in my last relationship eventually degenerated into an argument. The calls would start okay. I would ask my girlfriend how her day was and she would tell me. Yet no matter how hard we tried, the conversations could not help but turn to one of my favourite subjects: politics. Rather than debating our views objectively, we always made the conversations personal. No matter how hard we tried, they concluded with her crying and I being outraged. After awhile it didn't matter what the issue was, the conclusion was always the same. We couldn't go for minutes without having a full-blown argument. Communication between us collapsed and several months later the relationship was over.

Another thing that accompanied the phone arguments was an increase in the time between our visits. Unlike at the beginning, when we tried to see each other every two to three weeks, we started prolonging the time between our visits to months. Reasons such as homework or important social events at the university became easy excuses not to see each other. After all, what was the use? We probably would only argue anyway. It was this type of thinking that kept us apart, and made things even worse in the relationship by reducing the quality of communication time we had left for each other. The funny thing is that we never really realized what was going on until it was too late.

On the few occasions when I did see my girlfriend, it was like being with a stranger. We did everything in our power to avoid talking about serious issues because we knew they would only lead to arguments. We would go out together, hold hands, and make love, but we would never really talk about anything meaningful. Physically we were together, but emotionally we were miles apart, and we both felt it. The feelings of estrangement and detachment that usually accompanied the first few weeks of our becoming reacquainted, now lasted for our entire stay together. Apart from losing hope in my relationship, being with my girlfriend without being able to emotionally connect with her, was probably the saddest part of breaking up.

Some of our final conversations were not arguments, but they may as well have been. They usually revolved around how she wanted to travel around the world and how I wanted to return home to work. These discussions wouldn't have been so bad if our plans ended with us being together, but they never did. All they proved was that both of us had completely different goals that we wanted to pursue in completely different cities. Our conversations also revealed that neither of us was willing to compromise and if the relationship was going to work, one of us would have to give in and follow the other.

In reality, we probably could have continued without one of us subjugating the other. However, given our inability to communicate at the time, neither of us had a chance of realizing this. Neither one of us was willing to compromise, which combined with our emotional detachment, meant that our relationship had no possible future.

After enduring months of phone arguments, no physical or emotional contact with my girlfriend, and repeated discussions in which we concluded we would never be together, I gave up hope. For the first time, I felt that losing my girlfriend and possibly not finding someone else, was better than going through another day of suffering. Not surprisingly, a couple of days after I lost hope I phoned her and we agreed it was best to break up.

It still saddens me when I think of how long we went until we called it quits. I do not regret the experience, for now I know what the early signs are that a long-distance relationship is dissolving. My only wish is that I will not have to see those same clues again, for next to a death in the family or a severe illness, breaking up after being in a serious relationship for years, was one of the most traumatic experiences of my life.

Long-Distance Sex

S orry, there is no such thing.

Conclusion

One day a family member said, "Why don't you stop complaining about your long-distance relationships and write a book about them?" And that's exactly how it all started. I always wanted to write about a personal experience, so why not about my long-distance relationships? I had, after all, lived through two of them in a row. So instead of complaining my way through a third, I took my family's advice and started writing. I vowed that instead of missing Amanda, or complaining to my family, I would write, and write, and write. I would write until Amanda came home or I finished this book.

Well, Amanda hasn't come home yet, so I am going to have to start thinking about what to do on my weekends again. My poor family, instead of just reading about my relationship once a week (they helped me edit this book), will start hearing about it again.

Wait . . . I have an idea. To save myself and my family's sanity, I think a sequel is in order. It will be about a guy in a long-distance relationship who wrote a book, and at the end asked his readers for letters on their long-distance experiences. Are you with me so far? He received tons of letters and picked all of the interesting and inspiring stories that he combined with more of his own into another book called "Still Loving Your Long-Distance Relationship." So how about it? If you have something to share, write it down and send it to me. The best thing that could happen is your story appearing in my next book. The worst is that you could spend a few hours writing instead of missing your loved one.

Finally, if anyone tells you relationships are easy, especially long-distance ones, ignore them. They are full of it. It has been a struggle to maintain my relationships from day one. They take an abundance of time, effort, and love. I am not perfect by a longshot, making it a constant struggle to practice what I preach. Like everyone, I have done, and will do, things I regret in my relationship. It's only human. I am, however, committed to it, which gives me the desire to keep trying, to keep feeling happy, and not to lose hope whatever the circumstances. I think this type of commitment is the common ingredient in all successful relationships.

On that note, all I can say is stay strong! Although being in a long-distance relationship will seem difficult at times, if you believe in yourself and your relationship, you're 99% of the way there. If all else fails, write your feelings down---it works for me.

Until we talk again, take care.

- Stephen

P.S. You can mail me directly through my website at www.sblake.com, or write to me at the following address:

Stephen Blake
c/o Anton Publishing
305 Madison Ave.
Suite 1166
New York, New York 10165